CONFRONTING
THE
QUEEN OF HEAVEN

C. PETER WAGNER

D0921382

Confronting the Queen of Heaven
Copyright © 1998 by C. Peter Wagner
ISBN 0-9667481-3-1

Published by
Wagner Institute for Practical Ministry
P.O. Box 62958
Colorado Springs, CO 80962-2958

TABLE OF CONTENTS

INTRODUCTION

The body of Christ has come to a place today unlike anything known in church history. Even the Book of Acts has not recorded the kinds of awesome ministry we are now seeing in many parts of the world.

It seems as if Habakkuk 1:5 is literally coming true in our day:

> *Look among the nations and watch—*
> *Be utterly astounded!*
> *For I will work a work in your days*
> *Which you would not believe,*
> *though it were told you.*

Should we not expect this? After all, Jesus said, "He who believes in Me, the works that I do he will do also; and greater works than these will he do, because I go to My Father" (Jn. 14:12).

We live in the time of the greatest harvest of souls that the world has ever seen; awesome reports of supernatural power pour in from virtually every nation; the body of Christ is more unified than it has been in millennia; more people are praying and praying "in one accord" than ever before; and we live in the first generation ever to see light at the end of the tunnel of the Great Commission. What an incredible time to be a Christian!

THE DECADE OF SPIRITUAL WARFARE

Never before has God entrusted to His church the level of spiritual warfare which is occurring in every continent in the 1990s. Even ten years ago, we did not even have the vocabulary to describe what is almost commonplace these days, such as strategic-level spiritual warfare, spiritual mapping, identificational repentance, and prayer evangelism. The issue of divine timing raises the question as to why God would have waited until now to release the church for such a massive assault on the kingdom of Satan.

I believe the answer to this crucial question lies in the fact that in the 1990s the authentic government of the universal church has, once again, come into place. During the 1980s the prophetic ministry rose up within the church and began to assume its rightful position in the life and ministry of God's people. In the 1990s apostles began to appear and be legitimately recognized by the churches. We read in Ephesians that "[Jesus] gave some to be apostles, some prophets, some evangelists, and some pastors and teachers" (Eph. 4:11). The traditional church has received the ministry of evangelists, pastors, and teachers for centuries, but only recently has it also accepted prophets and apostles. However, because apostles and prophets are now operative, God is entrusting His church with high-level assignments that we have not previously seen.

In 1990, I had the privilege of helping to found the International Spiritual Warfare Network, and I have served as the international coordinator ever since. This has given me a ring side seat to watch the unfolding of God's plan for His spiritual army. In the early days, we were floundering, making our share of mistakes. But through the mentoring of the Holy Spirit we have learned rapidly, and now we are much more mature and prepared for battle. We have seen tremendous victories for the kingdom of God in the 1990s, particularly among the unreached peoples of the 10/40 Window.

Now, in the closing years of the decade and the millennium, God is entrusting us with a new level of spiritual warfare. Some of the things described in this booklet have not been common knowledge. This is not Spiritual Warfare 101. The new assignment that God has given to the International Spiritual Warfare Network and to the body of Christ in general deals with the highest levels of "rulers of the darkness of this age" as the Apostle Paul would say (see Eph. 6:12). The notion of confronting the Queen of Heaven is not fun and games. It is an advanced, high-risk assault against the powers of evil that no one would want to undertake other than by a direct command of God.

Why would anyone in their right mind want to take on high-ranking principalities and powers of darkness? Very simply, it is because of heaven and hell. God has given us the ministry of reconciliation. He has given us the gospel of Christ which is the power of God to salvation. He is not willing that any should perish. And, yet, not enough people are being saved. More often than not, evangelism gets bogged down. The light of the gospel does not shine as brightly as we know it should. Why? Paul tells us that it is because "the god of this age" has blinded the minds of unbelievers (see 2 Cor. 4:4).

Some think that there is not much that we can do about this. But there is. Paul says that "we are not ignorant of [Satan's] devices" (2 Cor. 2:11). God has given us the shield of faith and the sword of the Spirit (see Eph. 6:16-17). We are ready for battle as soon as the Commander-in-Chief gives us the word to go forth.

He has now given us the word to confront the Queen of Heaven. This booklet will tell how that command was received and how God expects His army to move into battle.

CHAPTER ONE

EPHESUS YESTERDAY AND TODAY

The major focal point for the Spiritual Warfare Network in our days has become the city of Ephesus in Turkey. Undoubtedly, other significant focal points will emerge as we come before God's throne and listen carefully to His voice as He speaks to us, but Turkey will be on center stage. For many years, Christians all over the world have prayed for God's blessing to be poured out on Turkey and on the Turkish people. Turkey is a beautiful land, a jewel of God's creation. Our Christian faith has deep roots in Turkey. Our desire is to see God's purpose for that land come to full fruition, and this is why I am advocating that we increase both the quantity and the fervency of our prayers for Turkey, proclaiming God's deep love for the Turks.

Why is Turkey, particularly the city of Ephesus, so important at this hinge of history? In order to explain, let's look at Ephesus yesterday, and then at Ephesus today.

EPHESUS YESTERDAY

Ephesus was once the center of world Christianity. Back in the days of the apostles, Ephesus was the third largest city in the

Roman Empire, boasting a population of 250,000. Only Rome and Alexandria were larger. It was a beautiful city of amazing art and architecture, a good deal of which has been restored by modern archaeologists. It was a port city, with bustling and lucrative commerce. A public bath house was located at every gate to the city, and no one was admitted without taking a complete bath. Ephesus was a center of education with schools, libraries and lecture halls. The homes of the well-to-do were fitted with indoor plumbing including hot and cold running water. A hospital was located near the center of the city. The awesome outdoor amphitheater seated 25,000 persons who could hear the voices on the stage without amplification.

The apostle Paul was the missionary whom God chose to take the gospel of Christ to Ephesus, at that time the capital city of the Roman province, Asia Minor. In Ephesus, Paul saw more fruit for his labor than in any other place he ever visited as a missionary. The Book of Acts reports that "[Paul preached the kingdom of God] for two years, so that all who dwelt in Asia heard the word of the Lord Jesus, both Jews and Greeks" (Acts 19:10); and, while Paul was there "the word of the Lord grew mighty and prevailed" (Acts 19:20). That would be like a missionary arriving in Chicago and, two years later, being able to say, "All Illinois has heard the gospel!"

SPIRITUAL WARFARE AND UNUSUAL MIRACLES

What was Paul doing during those two years? He was basically engaged in spiritual warfare, practicing what John Wimber would have called "power evangelism." There was so much supernatural power being released through Paul and others, that "God worked unusual miracles by the hands of Paul" (Acts 19:11). I love to read those words! Apparently there was so much power that a distinction needed to be made between "usual" and "unusual" miracles. We are seeing similar things today in places like China and Argentina.

There are three important levels of spiritual warfare, all of which were taking place in Ephesus. The first level is *ground-level spiritual warfare*, which means casting demons out of individuals. This is what Jesus commanded His disciples to do when He sent them out saying, "As you go, preach, saying, 'The kingdom of heaven is at hand.' Heal the sick, cast out demons" (Mt. 10:7-8).

Ordinarily, God heals the sick and drives out demons when Christian people minister directly to individuals, lay hands on them, anoint them with oil, and pray for them and their specific needs. Those are the "usual" miracles. But in Ephesus there was so much power that "even handkerchiefs or aprons were brought from [Paul's] body to the sick, and the diseases left them and the evil spirits went out of them" (Acts 19:12). No wonder the adjective "unusual" is used here!

THE MAGICIANS AND THEIR BONFIRE

The second level of spiritual warfare is *occult-level spiritual warfare*. This means dealing with powers of darkness that are more coordinated and organized than one or more demons who might happen to be afflicting a certain person at a certain time. We can think of this as witchcraft or Satanism or fortune-telling or shamanism or New Age or Freemasonry or Tibetan Buddhism or other occult practices.

Ephesus, in the days of Paul, was a center of magic. According to information taken from Clinton Arnold's excellent book, *Ephesians: Power and Magic* (Baker Books), Ephesus could have been regarded as the center of magic in the Roman Empire. It would have attracted the most famous magicians, as well as those who wanted to learn the trade from them. Paul ministered to the magicians in Ephesus with outstanding results. In order to win these power brokers to Christ, there must have been numerous power encounters clearly demonstrating that the power of God was greater than any of the supernatural powers of darkness that the magicians were in touch with.

We read that "Many of those who had practiced magic brought their books together and burned them in the sight of all. And they counted up the value of them, and it totaled fifty thousand pieces of silver" (Acts 19:19). When I researched this for my commentary on Acts, I calculated that in the U.S. economy today, the pile of magic paraphernalia that was burned would have been worth $4 million!

THE TERRITORIAL SPIRIT: DIANA OF THE EPHESIANS

The third, and highest level of spiritual warfare is *strategic-level spiritual warfare.* This involves confrontation with the high-ranking territorial spirits which have been assigned by Satan to coordinate the activities of the kingdom of darkness over a certain area in order to keep the people's minds blinded to the "gospel of the glory of Christ" as we read in 2 Corinthians 4:3-4. Paul refers to this when he says, "We do not wrestle against flesh and blood, but against principalities, against powers, against the rulers of the darkness of this age" (Eph. 6:12).

The chief territorial spirit over Ephesus and Asia Minor was the renowned Diana of the Ephesians (also known by her Greek name, Artemis). Some historians believe that she might have been the most worshipped deity of the whole Roman Empire at the time. Her temple in Ephesus was listed as one of the Seven Wonders of the Ancient World, the most outstanding and opulent example of architecture in the whole city. Offerings and sacrifices were made to this demonic power year round. Her followers called her "magnificent" and "great goddess" and "savior" and "Queen of Heaven." Before Paul arrived, she had things very well in hand in the greater Ephesus area and beyond.

But then, confusion set in. The demons, who were supposed to be under her authority, were being driven out of people they had oppressed for years by mere handkerchiefs! The magicians, presumably her most elite troops, were deserting the kingdom of darkness by droves, and entering the kingdom of this "Jesus" whom Paul was preaching. Diana had never seen anything like this before! Her armies were retreating in chaos. She was rapidly losing the authority over Ephesus that she had maintained for centuries.

Diana's power was being neutralized so much by the gospel that the common people began to notice. They stopped worshipping her, sacrificing to her, and purchasing her idols. By the time Paul's two years of ministry were coming to a close, the silversmiths, who were manufacturing these idols, were going out of business, so they staged a public riot. They filled the huge amphitheater and shouted for two hours, "Great is Diana of the Ephesians" (Acts 19:34).

THE AIR WAR AND THE GROUND WAR

Paul's strategic-level spiritual warfare was like the air war of modern military strategy. No responsible commander would send in ground troops unless the air war had been won. It would be suicide. This is why Paul made sure that Diana had been weakened before he sent his church planters all through the city of Ephesus and the province of Asia Minor. Actually, Paul did not personally plant the churches in Asia Minor (seven of which are mentioned in Revelation 2 and 3). He trained church planters in the "school of Tyrannus," a school building that he rented, and sent them out as ground troops (see Acts 19:9-10).

DIANA'S DEMISE

By the time Paul left Ephesus, Diana had been severely battered and weakened. But she wasn't yet taken out of the picture. Paul never confronted her one-on-one or entered her temple to do direct strategic-level spiritual warfare. The silversmiths accused him of doing this, but they couldn't make their charges stick in court. Diana lost much power because of Paul's aggressive spiritual warfare on the ground level and on the occult level. The kingdom of darkness is all connected, and what happens on any one of the three levels affects the other levels and the whole realm of Satan.

God chose the apostle John to do the final assault. Subsequent history, not the Book of Acts, tells us that a few years after Paul left, John moved to Ephesus and finished his career there. Ramsay MacMullen, a well-known historian on the faculty of Yale University, provides us with some very interesting details of John's ministry in Ephesus in the area of strategic-level spiritual warfare. MacMullen, a specialist in the history of the Roman Empire, has written a scholarly treatise called *The Christianization of the Roman Empire 100-400* (Yale University Press). In it, he argues that the principal factor for converting the Roman Empire to Christianity was casting out demons. He gives many examples of spiritual warfare in his book.

One of them is the story of the apostle John and his one-on-one confrontation with Diana of the Ephesians. MacMullen, citing historical sources, says that John, unlike Paul, did go into Diana's temple to do spiritual warfare. He says, "In the very temple of [Diana herself], [John] prayed, 'O God . . . at whose name every idol takes flight and every demon and every unclean power: now let the demon that is here [in this temple] take flight at thy name . . .' And while John was saying this, all of a sudden the altar of [Diana] split in many pieces . . . and half the temple fell down" (p. 26).

MacMullen goes on to say that this power encounter brought multitudes of Ephesians to faith in Christ. Then he comments, as a professional historian, on why he believes that this, along with similar instances in the evangelization of the Roman Empire, should be accepted as historically valid.

Within about 50 years after this hardly anyone in the Roman Empire worshipped Diana any more. Her cult was reduced to a mere shadow of what it had been before Paul and John went to Ephesus. And the city of Ephesus became the center of world Christianity for the next 200 years.

EPHESUS TODAY

In August 1997, Doris and I made our first trip to Turkey as a part of the Praying Through the Window III initiative that we were helping to coordinate. God had laid it on our hearts to choose the Turks as the unreached people group on which we would concentrate our prayers. This was new ground for us since we had very little previous knowledge of Turkey and no Turkish personal friends.

We were delighted with what we found. Turkey is a beautiful

country with as long a history as any nation in the world. Some say that the Garden of Eden was located in Turkey, and that could well be the case. The people are wonderful—friendly, hospitable, easy-going, industrious. We understood why Turkey would be one of the preferred tourist destinations for vacationing Europeans. When we left, we wanted to go back again.

Most Turks are Muslims, and they have an inbred loyalty to their faith. But the Turkish government is a secular government, strongly resisting attempts by Islamic fundamentalists to impose the kind of closed society seen in many Middle Eastern lands. Turks are not Arabs, nor do they ever want to be. They want to be part of the European Union. Christian churches and Bible schools and bookstores and religious pilgrimages are allowed. Turks are free to convert to Christianity if they so desire. There are something like 500 born-again believers in Turkey today. True, there are some laws restricting the ways evangelism can be carried out and prohibiting public distribution of literature, but they apply to Christians and non-Christians alike. Christians who intentionally disobey these laws deserve punishment.

THE MOON GODDESS

While we were in Turkey we learned something that we were not previously aware of. The ancient Moon Goddess (sometimes referred to in literature by the masculine "Moon God") has exerted a good bit of influence over peoples of the Middle East for millennia. The spiritual powers behind moon worship, whether personified as male or female (human gender distinctions are not known to have parallels among angelic beings), have been more deeply embedded in many Middle Eastern cultures (as well as many cultures outside of the Middle East) than we have usually thought. The symbol of the Moon Goddess is the crescent moon.

Did the Moon Goddess have anything to do with Diana of the Ephesians? I had seen pictures of the many-breasted statue of Diana numerous times, but it was only during this visit to Turkey that I noticed that her necklace is the crescent moon! The Moon Goddess relates to biblical history. Both Ur of the Chaldeans, where Abraham's family came from, and Haran, where Abraham lived until his father died, were cities ruled over by the Moon Goddess, Sin. Abraham's family worshipped the Moon Goddess, so it would not be an exaggeration to suppose that Abraham himself was a convert from the Moon Goddess to Jahweh!

THE QUEEN OF HEAVEN

The principality of darkness manifesting in the form of both the Moon Goddess and Diana of the Ephesians is the Queen of Heaven. One of the names of Diana was "Queen of Heaven."

Who is the Queen of Heaven?

Quite possibly, the only place in the Bible where God emphatically tells His followers *not* to pray for certain other people is Jeremiah 7:16: "Do not pray for this people, nor lift up a cry or prayer for them, nor make intercession to Me; for I will not hear you." This is an extraordinary statement reflecting a situation which apparently demands that God's attribute of wrath overshadow His attribute of mercy. Something really bad must be happening to provoke such a response. What is it?

It involves the Queen of Heaven. "The children gather wood, the fathers kindle the fire, and the women knead their dough to make cakes for the queen of heaven" (Jer. 7:18). Whole families, men, women and children, are involved in worshipping this unclean territorial spirit of evil. God goes on to say that "they provoke Me to anger." An even longer passage comes up in Jeremiah 44 where the Jews in Egypt were "[burning] incense to the queen of heaven and [pouring] out drink offerings to her" (Jer. 44:17). God pleads, "Oh, do not do this abominable thing that I hate!" (Jer. 44:4).

In fact, it was because the Jews in Jerusalem and Judah had been doing that very same thing that God sent them to the seventy years of Babylonian captivity (this is explained in Jeremiah 44:2-3).

The Great Harlot on Many Waters

Because God is a God who is not willing that any should perish (see 2 Peter 3:9), my hypothesis is that He hates the Queen of Heaven so much because she is the demonic principality who is most responsible under Satan for keeping unbelievers in spiritual darkness. It could well be that more people are in Hell today because of the influence of the Queen of Heaven than because of any other spiritual influence.

The Queen of Heaven is "the great harlot who sits on many waters" in Revelation 17. What are the "waters"? "The waters which you saw, where the harlot sits, are peoples, multitudes, nations, and tongues" (Rev. 17:15).

Why have many unreached peoples been impervious to receiving the great blessing that God desires to pour out upon them and upon their nations? Because of the deceptive power of the Queen of Heaven. It is now time to take spiritual action!

CHAPTER TWO

HOW SHOULD
WE RESPOND?

When Paul left Ephesus, the church he left behind (which was not a large downtown church as we might think, but numerous house churches scattered across the city and throughout the province of Asia Minor) was flourishing. The principalities and powers of darkness had been pushed back and the kingdom of God was thoroughly rooted in the area.

About five or six years later Paul wrote a letter to the believers in Ephesus from a Roman prison. It should not surprise us that The Epistle of Paul to the Ephesians would contain a higher percentage of power terminology than any other book in the New Testament. The spiritual warfare that had helped the church take root there was continuing. By that time Timothy had gone to minister in Ephesus, and that is why Paul would write to Timothy such things as: "wage the good warfare" (1 Tim. 1:18); "fight the good fight" (1 Tim. 6:12); "endure hardship as a good soldier of Jesus Christ" (2 Tim. 2:3); and "no one engaged in warfare entangles himself with the affairs of this life" (2 Tim. 2:4). Then soon after Timothy left, John went to Ephesus and we have already seen some of the spiritual warfare that he engaged in, especially in the temple of Diana.

Undoubtedly, as he was writing Ephesians, Paul would have been replaying in his mind the amazing demonic deliverances through handkerchiefs, his power encounters with the magicians, and the silversmiths' riot in the huge amphitheater. It was Paul's desire that what had been gained through spiritual warfare would be maintained through spiritual warfare. That is why, if we now feel it is time to do battle against the Queen of Heaven once again, we would expect to receive important guidelines from the Book of Ephesians.

Let's see what Ephesians says.

THE TRUE NATURE OF THE BATTLE

Territorial spirits such as the Queen of Heaven should not be on the spiritual throne of nations like Turkey or like Japan where she rules as the Sun Goddess or like Mexico where she is known as the Virgin of Guadalupe or like Nepal where she is Sagarmatha or of cities like Calcutta where she is disguised as Cali. Jesus Christ should be on the throne. It is only when darkness is pushed back and the light of the gospel comes that the full blessing of God will be poured out on nations and on their people.

When Paul writes to the believers in Ephesus, he tells them he is praying "that the God of our Lord Jesus Christ, the Father of glory, may give to you the spirit of wisdom and revelation" (Eph. 1:17). Before we do spiritual warfare on any level, but particularly on the strategic-level, revelation is absolutely necessary. We must hear from God and allow Him to reveal Himself and His will to us. Then we need wisdom to know how to interpret what we hear and how to act on God's commands. Revelation without wisdom can lead us into foolishness. Wisdom without revelation can lead us down a dead-end street.

"ON EARTH IS NOT HIS EQUAL"

This wisdom and revelation is not wisdom and revelation in general. It specifically relates to what Paul describes as "the exceeding greatness of [God's] power toward us who believe, according to the working of His mighty power" (Eph. 1:19). Tapping into God's power is essential. Only those who are suicidal should go into spiritual warfare trusting on their human abilities. Martin Luther, in his magnificent spiritual warfare song, "A Mighty Fortress Is Our God," mentions the devil and then says, "On earth is not his equal." This is so true! Only the mighty power of God can support us as we move aggressively against the forces of darkness.

What level of spiritual warfare does Paul have in mind as he writes to the Ephesians? He says that Jesus is on the right hand of God and "far above all principality and power and might and dominion" (Eph. 1:21). Undoubtedly, Diana of the Ephesians and the daily sacrifices in her ornate temple are in Paul's mind. Jesus is superior to Diana and to all similar territorial spirits, no matter how long they have ruled people groups or cities. The armies of God are being called forth to enforce the rightful rule of the King of kings and Lord of lords on the highest spiritual levels!

All this is in Chapter 1 of Ephesians. Throughout the epistle Paul continues to set other pieces and conditions in order, until he gets to his close in Chapter 6 where he declares, among other things, that "we do not wrestle against flesh and blood, but against principalities, against powers, against the rulers of the darkness of this age" (Eph. 6:12). This, clearly, is strategic-level spiritual warfare.

THE BODY TAKES ORDERS FROM THE HEAD

Paul reminds the Ephesians that God has designated Jesus as "the head over all things to the church, which is His body, the fullness of Him who fills all in all" (Eph. 1:22-23).

If believers, in any aspect of their lives, want to be in the place that God wants them to be, they must submit to the head of the body, Jesus Christ. This applies to individuals in particular, but also to the church in general. It becomes extremely important for effective spiritual warfare.

The analogy of the head and the body is so simple that it surprises me when I find those who do not seem to catch on. Let's make the application by beginning with our own human bodies. We have a head and we have a body. The head directs the rest of the body. The body carries out the will of the head.

For example, suppose I set out to build a house. My head tells me to build a house and what kind of a house and where it should be located. But my head doesn't build the house, my body does. My head might tell me to cook a meal, but my head doesn't cook the meal, my body does. My head tells me to drive a car, but heads don't drive cars.

THE HEAD SAYS: "ATTACK THE ENEMY!"

Since Jesus is the head of the body of Christ, we must follow His directions. He will tell us what action to take, but He Himself doesn't intend to take the action because He is the head. There are at least three very important things that the head is telling the body about spiritual warfare, all related to the city of Ephesus.

1. Stand against the wiles of the devil.

Paul tells the Ephesians to put on the whole armor of God "that you may be able to stand against the wiles of the devil" (Eph. 6:13). This is not a benign command. It is not something which is easy to do. The reason is that this devil is an awesome being. Paul, in the same epistle, calls him "the prince of the power of the air" (Eph. 2:2). It is hard for me to understand why some Christian leaders insist on trivializing Satan's power. Referring to him as a wimp or as a toothless lion only serves to embolden people to think they can get away with attacking the devil with a fly swatter.

I suspect that by saying things like this, they are comparing the power of the devil to the power of God, and it is true that there is no contest between the two of them. But this is not the scenario. We are not spectators watching a fight between God and demons. We are the ones to stand against the wiles of the devil.

The head tells the body to do it, and the head is not going to do it for us.

2. Engage in proactive spiritual warfare.

The epistle that Paul wrote to the Ephesians isn't the only letter to the church in Ephesus that we find in the New Testament. The other one is found in Revelation 2:1-7, and it was composed by the head of the church Himself. All seven letters in Revelation 2 and 3 were written by Jesus to the church in Ephesus and the other churches in Asia Minor which Paul's team had planted.

In each of these letters Jesus says that those who have ears should hear what the Holy Spirit is saying to the churches. The only other command-type verb found in all seven is "to overcome." And each time it is used, it is accompanied with an extravagant promise. In the letter to Ephesus, for example, Jesus says, "To him who overcomes, I will give to eat from the tree of life which is in the midst of the Paradise of God" (Rev. 2:7).

The word "overcome" which Jesus repeats seven times is *nikao* in the original Greek. It is a military word meaning "to conquer" in secular Greek, but, according to The New International Dictionary of New Testament Theology: "In the New Testament [*nikao*] almost always presupposes the conflict between God and opposing demonic powers" (Vol. 1, p. 650). In other words, it means to do spiritual warfare.

BINDING THE STRONG MAN

Jesus uses the same word in Luke 11:22 when He talks about overcoming (*nikao*) the strong man in reference to Beelzebub, a high ranking principality in the order of the Queen of Heaven. The parallel passage in Matthew uses a different verb and speaks of "binding the strong man" (Mt. 12:29), the term more frequently used among those of the International Spiritual Warfare Network today.

Let's not miss the point. Seven times Jesus tells His followers to do spiritual warfare, and the kind of warfare that can be interpreted as strategic-level spiritual warfare. This was after the cross and the resurrection. I mention that because some think that Jesus' defeat of the powers of darkness on the cross (see Col. 2:15) has relieved us of any responsibility of doing proactive spiritual warfare ourselves. If it had, Jesus wouldn't have told us to do it seven times after He died on the cross. This is the head speaking to the body, and the body should submit to the directions of the head.

John, of course, was the scribe who heard the words from Jesus and wrote them in the text of the Book of Revelation. He wrote this during the time that he had been exiled from his home in Ephesus to the Island of Patmos under the persecution of the Roman emperor Domitian. Later, when Domitian died, John returned to Ephesus. Could I be pardoned for guessing (I admit that I have no proof) that it was after John had written about "overcoming" on Patmos that he returned to Ephesus and boldly moved into the power encounter in the temple of Diana of the Ephesians that we read about in the last chapter? It could well be.

3. Declare God's wisdom to the principalities.
Paul expresses to the Ephesians his burning desire that "the manifold wisdom of God might be made known by the church to the principalities and powers in the heavenly places" (Eph. 3:10). This is another one of the commands from the head of the body, and it explicitly says that the church should make this declaration to the powers in the invisible world. There are many interpretations as to what exactly this might mean, but one of them would be that we declare the gospel of the Kingdom of God.

The church, by deed and also by word, should remind the territorial spirits over places like Ephesus that the kingdom of God has invaded the kingdom of darkness beginning with the life, death, and resurrection of Jesus Christ, and that the god of this age will no longer blind the minds of unbelievers to the glorious gospel of Christ in Ephesus, in Turkey, in Japan, in Nepal, in Calcutta, or in any other place. This kind of a declaration of war will predictably spark negative reactions and counterattacks from the forces of evil and the spiritual battle will be engaged.

One of the major apostles of the extraordinary Argentine Revival, now in its fifteenth year, is evangelist Carlos Annacondia. In virtually every one of his meetings, he literally declares the wisdom of God to the devil and to any spiritual principalities that might be in the vicinity. Many times I have heard him do this in a very loud voice and with powerful anointing of the Holy Spirit. The title of his excellent new book is: *Listen to Me, Satan!* (Creation House). When this war cry goes forth, night after night, things begin to happen. Demons manifest and are summarily dispatched, sick people are healed miraculously, and sinners literally run to the platform to get saved. Over two million have been born again in his campaigns so far.

ANOTHER VERSE OF "KUMBAYA"?

One reason that this hasn't happened more in America is that the church has been too passive. I know churches that have decided to sit back and wait until Jesus does it. Some say that they prefer to be in the spiritual "bedroom" and enjoy intimacy with God through praise and worship, rather than go out to the "battle-field" where there might be casualties. Too many churches are sitting around singing another verse of "Kumbaya," while whole nations remain under the rule of territorial spirits and thousands are dying and going to hell every day. Rather than obeying the head, certain parts of the body of Christ seem to be waiting for the head to do the job for them. It doesn't usually happen that way.

Obviously, there is much to do right now that we haven't been doing in the past. In order to do the right things, we need that spirit of wisdom and revelation that Paul was praying for. What is the Holy Spirit saying to the churches today? How is the head trying to direct the body of Christ? I believe that we have some of the answers to those crucial questions.

CHAPTER THREE

THE CHALLENGE
OF THE QUEEN OF HEAVEN

One of the first responsibilities I had when I took the position of coordinator of the International Spiritual Warfare Network in 1990 was to visit the different regions of the world and meet with those who understood at least something about strategic-level spiritual warfare and who were attempting to practice it to one degree or another. Since so much of this was new to me back in the early 1990s, I most frequently took the role of a listener and a learner. It didn't take long to begin to recognize that one discernible pattern from continent to continent was frequent references to the "Queen of Heaven."

So I began to ask questions about the Queen of Heaven. The Bible tells us that if we are ignorant of the wiles of the devil, he will then take advantage of us (see 2 Cor. 2:11).

What are the wiles of the Queen of Heaven? By now I was beginning to realize that she must be one of the most important principalities under the command of Satan, but what was her modus operandi? For years all I could get were unrelated bits and pieces, but I had no question that some day God would show us the answer. I now believe that one reason we did not arrive at an international consensus is that God knew we were not yet ready and that He Himself was directing the timing.

THE RECONCILIATION WALK

When Doris and I did our prayer journey to Turkey in August 1997, we had no inkling that it would be anything more than our field participation in the Praying Through the Window III initiative. We expected to pray God's blessing on the Turkish people and come home. We had taken vacation time to do this, so we also planned a couple of days of vacation on the same trip. We had not given any particular thought or prayer to issues relating to the Queen of Heaven before we left. We had sensed, however, that we should make a hotel reservation in Izmir in order to pray in Ephesus and Pergamum.

But on the way we planned to stop in Istanbul for a few days in order to encourage and to pray with the intercessors who were participating in the Reconciliation Walk. I now see that the Reconciliation Walk was a principal factor in God's timing for a confrontation with the Queen of Heaven.

The Reconciliation Walk, a vision of YWAM's Lynn Green, is the most massive prayer expedition of the decade. The design is very simple: mobilize Christian intercessors to walk every known route of the First Crusade with only one agenda item: repenting (or apologizing) to Muslims and Jews for the sins which our Christian ancestors committed against them in the First Crusade 900 years ago, and in the subsequent crusades.

ASKING FORGIVENESS FOR THE CRUSADES

Our collective Christian memory of the medieval crusades is very dim. We tend to think that they are ancient history—long gone and forgotten. We have trivialized the crusades so much that we even call some of our current evangelistic efforts "crusades," as if what our ancestors did was benign or even noble.

Muslims and Jews have different memories. For them the crusades might as well have taken place yesterday. In school they are taught to interpret Christians and Christianity, at least partially, in light of the crusades. They learn, among other things, that when the Christian crusaders entered Jerusalem at the finale of the First Crusade in July of 1099, they massacred 30,000 defenseless Muslim civilians, including women and children, in cold blood. They learn that the 6,000 Jews who lived in Jerusalem at the time fled to their synagogue and packed themselves in, thinking that they would be safe. But the crusaders bolted the doors from the outside and set fire to the synagogue. As the Jews were burning to death in this 11th century holocaust, the crusaders were riding their horses around the synagogue under banners embroidered with the Christian cross, drowning out the screams of the dying by singing Christian hymns.

Fortunately, through leaders like John Dawson and Cindy Jacobs and Lynn Green and others, we now know that we Christians who are living today can do something about a situation like this through identificational repentance. The wounds of the past can be healed if we humble ourselves, pray, seek God's face, and turn from our wicked ways as we read in 2 Chronicles 7:14. The Reconciliation Walk is intended to be a giant step in this direction. There is no stronghold keeping the full blessing of God from being poured out on Muslims greater than that caused by the crusades, and the Reconciliation Walk, through public actions of humility and repentance, is attempting to tear down this stronghold of darkness.

I had the privilege of being in Cologne, Germany on Easter Sunday 1996 to help commission the first group of intercessors undertaking the Reconciliation Walk. This was the 900th anniversary of the day that Peter the Hermit led his troops into the First Crusade. Our visit to Istanbul in August 1997 occurred at the midpoint of the expedition. And Doris and I hope to be present to receive the intercessors when they finish in Jerusalem in July 1999.

THE FAX FROM ALICE SMITH

Before we left Istanbul, Doris and I did not know just how we were to pray at Ephesus and at Pergamum. But we unexpectedly received a three-page fax sent to the hotel from Alice Smith, our I-1 intercessor who lives in Houston, Texas. Alice is one of an inner circle of 22 personal intercessors who pray fervently for Doris and me and who frequently hear from the Lord for us. I like to say that I do hear from God myself, but half the time I need a hearing aid! This time, Alice was the spiritual hearing aid.

Alice said, as I recall, that she had been praying for us from something like 2:00 am to 5:00 am. Such a thing was not altogether unusual—it had happened before. But this time, the Lord showed her how Doris and I were to pray at the temple of Diana in Ephesus and at the seat of Satan (see Rev. 2:13) in Pergamum. So we did. We contracted a personal tour guide and prayed in Ephesus one morning and the same afternoon in Pergamum, following the script that God had given to us in the fax.

Alice said, drawing from Revelation 2:17, that while in Pergamum I would receive hidden manna, a white stone, and a new name. The white stone is now in my study in Colorado Springs. I think I know what the new name is, but I am not supposed to tell anyone, according to that scripture. But, most significantly, she said that the "hidden manna" would be *new revelation concerning an important step toward world evangelization*. Doris and I took that literally, and so we were prepared to receive any directions that the Lord would give us on this trip. The importance of this prayer journey now had a new meaning!

SPIRITUAL ELECTRICITY IN EPHESUS!

Our first stop was Ephesus. We toured the ancient city, but when we came to the temple of Diana we asked our Muslim tour guide to let us go to the site by ourselves because we wanted to do some Christian praying. The temple area is a mess—it has not been restored like many other parts of ancient Ephesus. Very few other tourists were around.

As we crossed the boundary of the temple facility itself, Doris' body turned into electricity! For years she has had a ministry of demonic deliverance, so she has developed an above average sensitivity to things like this. There was no mistake. "The power is still here!" she said. We thought this was strange, because it did not look as if Diana's altar was in current use for worship or sacrifices or the like. It was only later that we came to believe that the central power point is probably not precisely in the temple ruins, but in a nearby site. More on that later.

When we prayed at the seat of Satan (the altar of Zeus) in Pergamum, Doris did not feel the same presence of the powers of darkness. Perhaps that is because the altar had been carried to Germany and reconstructed in the Pergamum Museum in Berlin. Hitler was said to have looked to that altar for much of the occult power he used to create the Third Reich.

MARY, THE MOTHER OF JESUS, IN EPHESUS

When the Apostle John went to Ephesus, he took Mary, Jesus' mother. Looking down from the cross, Jesus had said to Mary, "Woman, behold your son!" Then He had said to John, "Behold your mother!" And "from that hour that disciple [John] took her to his own home" (Jn. 19:25-27). Some say that Mary died. Some say she was taken directly to heaven like Elijah. However she might have left the earth, the last place she was seen alive was in Ephesus.

So much is history. Now I am switching into a "what if"? Would it be unreasonable to suppose that something like this might have gone through the mind of the Queen of Heaven? Could it be that the Queen of Heaven skillfully executed what George Otis, Jr. would call a "deceptive adaptation"? After Paul and John ministered in Ephesus, the cult of Diana had gone into a tailspin. Ephesus became the world center of Christianity. From that time on, the Queen of Heaven would have no more use for Diana. But her assignment from Satan was still to keep people in spiritual darkness.

So could it be that the Queen of Heaven began to ask herself whether, since she had been unsuccessful in stopping Christianity from the outside, there might be a way to keep people from being saved from the inside? But how? By now the true Mary is in heaven with her Son. Would it be possible to fabricate a counterfeit Mary within Christianity who could be empowered by the Queen of Heaven to do miracles and make appearances, and thus attract the worship, even in Christian churches, that should be given only to Jesus Christ? There might be a way to transfer the power that was once in Diana to the counterfeit Mary, right there in the city of Ephesus. If people won't worship Diana, let's see if they will worship a false Mary!

I want it understood by all that I am using the term "counterfeit Mary" to distinguish her from the real Mary, the mother of Jesus. The true Mary is blessed among women, as the angel Gabriel declared (see Lk. 1:28). There never has been nor will there ever be another woman to match her. Because God highly favored her, we also must highly favor and honor her. She is now in heaven with her Son. The Bible gives us no details of what she might be doing, but I can well believe that she would be appalled at what the Queen of Heaven has been getting away with here on earth in her assignment from Satan to keep people blinded to Jesus and His love.

THE MOTHER OF GOD

As history progressed, the center of Christianity gradually moved from Ephesus to Rome and Constantinople. As this happened, and as the Roman Empire was declared Christian by Emperor Constantine, the counterfeit Mary began to be drawn more and more into the center of Christian liturgy and worship. This progressed to such a point that the church in Rome decided to declare officially that Mary was the "Mother of God."

How should this be done? Why not go back to Ephesus itself? In A.D. 431, a so-called "ecumenical council" was convened in Ephesus. The Council of Ephesus declared that Mary was the *Theotokos,* the Mother of God. The dogma remains in the Roman church even today.

IDOL WORSHIP IN EPHESUS

In Ephesus a shrine was constructed to house an idol of the counterfeit Mary. Now, while there may be relatively little overt worship at the altar of Diana of the Ephesians, Mary's idol is actively worshipped 365 days a year with candles, gifts of flowers and other things. Devotees bow down, honor her, and pray to her as if she were somehow going to transmit their prayers to Jesus. There is little thought that the Queen of Heaven might be around to short-circuit those prayers. This idol shrine is presumably the physical site where the power that Doris felt in Ephesus is located today.

When Doris and I took a guided tour of the Vatican in Rome a few years ago, we had a hard time trying to understand why a life-sized statue of Diana of the Ephesians should be located in a room in the Vatican along with statues of Christian saints. After visiting Ephesus, we think we have a better idea as to why.

Mary Is Called "Queen of Heaven"

It is interesting that many of the pictures of the Virgin Mary have her standing either on the crescent moon, or with the crescent moon encircling her head. Others have a crown on her head, and one of her official designations is "Queen of Heaven." For example, few people know that the full original Spanish name of the city of Los Angeles is "The City (*Pueblo*) of Our Lady, Queen of the Angels (*Reina de los Angeles*). Some refer to L.A. as "the city of angels." It would be more accurate, however, to recognize it as "the city of the *queen* of the angels otherwise known as the Queen of Heaven."

How far the exaltation of this counterfeit Mary, empowered by the Queen of Heaven, will go is anyone's guess. Many were shocked when the August 25, 1997 *Newsweek* magazine reported that in the last four years the pope has received 4,340,429 signed petitions encouraging him to declare officially that the Virgin Mary is the "Co-Redemptrix" or co-redeemer with Christ. When the pope visited Cuba in 1998, he crowned the idol of the Virgin of Merced, declaring her Queen of Cuba. This happens to be the exact same idol which is worshipped by devotees of the Satanic Cuban cult known as *Santería*.

If the head, Jesus, is telling the body, the church, to overcome (*nikao*) and engage the powers of darkness in overt strategic-level spiritual warfare, what specifically should be done about the situation we have just described?

CHAPTER FOUR

OVERCOMING
THE QUEEN

All through the decade of the 1990s, prophetic intercession has been directed against major strongholds associated with the Queen of Heaven, much of it coordinated by the members of the Spiritual Warfare Network. I want us to keep in mind that the purpose of these prayer assaults has been to attempt to remove the spiritual blinders that the god of this age has wrapped around the minds of unbelievers on every continent. These actions are attempting to neutralize the power of the harlot over many waters, who commits fornication with kings, and who oppresses whole nations and people groups (see Rev. 17).

OPERATION ICE CASTLE

Ana Mendez is the coordinator of the Strategic Projects Task Force of the International Spiritual Warfare Network and also the regional coordinator for Southern Mexico. She is one of the most experienced and highly respected prophetic intercessors in our AD2000 prayer circles. She has taken prayer for the unreached peoples of the 10/40 Window so seriously that she established a 10/40 Window prayer tower in Mexico City, continually occupied by fervent intercessors.

One day, while in prayer in the 10/40 Window prayer tower, God showed Ana that a major stronghold of darkness over the whole 10/40 Window was located on the highest of high places, Mt. Everest in the Himalaya Mountains. At that moment, she knew that she was to lead a prayer journey to Mt. Everest. This was such an awesome challenge that she carefully researched the possibilities and sought confirmation from Rony Chavez of Costa Rica, one of Latin America's most widely recognized prophets and the person providing Ana's spiritual covering. She also consulted with Harold Caballeros, the Spiritual Warfare Network regional coordinator for the Spanish-speaking world, with Cindy Jacobs, coordinator of the U.S Spiritual Warfare Network, with Doris and me, and with others.

All agreed that she should do it, under the condition that everyone who participated would be fully conscious of the physical, emotional, and spiritual risks associated with such a high level (both topographically and spiritually speaking) prayer assault. As Doris prayed about it, she felt that God was calling her to join the expedition, despite crippling arthritis for which three total joint replacements would be required when she got back home. Rony Chavez assumed the apostolic responsibility for the expedition and volunteered to go with the team to the Mt. Everest base camp. All together, twenty-six intercessors from Mexico, Costa Rica, Colombia, United States and Viet Nam flew into Kathmandu, Nepal, and then continued to Mt. Everest. This was September 1997.

Part of God's call to Ana in the prayer tower was showing her a vision of the Himalayas as a huge castle made of ice, in which each of the surrounding mountain peaks housed high-ranking demonic spirits. That is why we labeled the project "Operation Ice Castle." How would this relate to confronting the Queen of Heaven? Mt. Everest is the British name for the highest mountain in the world. Its original name in Nepali, known and used today by the natives, is Sagarmatha, Mother of the Universe!

Across the border in Tibet, it is called Chomolugma, which means the same thing.

PRAYING IN THE HIMALAYAS

Some of the intercessors, including Doris, prayed for three weeks in the Everest View Hotel, with no hot water, at 13,000 feet. Others prayed at the Everest Base Camp at 18,000 feet, where we came within a whisker of losing a brother through cerebral edema. Ana's team, which had taken professional alpine training in Mexico and Peru before leaving, scaled the ice cliffs and crossed bottomless crevasses, climbing to 20,000 feet.

Ana said, "Our assignment from God was to take down the foundations of The Great Babylon, the harlot over many waters, which supported the false religious systems of the world. He clearly showed us where we should go for our prophetic act by revealing a large, brown stone formation, completely surrounded by walls of ice resembling a castle, and shaped exactly like an idol of the Queen of Heaven. This seat of the Mother of the Universe was 20,000 feet high, and to get there we had to cross the ice fall, the most dangerous part of the Everest ascent, with no guide but Him and no help from other than angels."

This prophetic act, as well as others, was recorded on video tape. Several unmistakable signs in the natural world confirmed that it had been a successful venture and that it had deeply affected the invisible world. If not the strongest, it would be seen as one of the strongest assaults on the Queen of Heaven ever undertaken. Among other things, it helped clear the spiritual way for the following month, October 1997, the climaxe of the Praying Through the Window III event sponsored by the AD2000 United Prayer Track. It was a very important precursor of Operation Queen's Palace.

Very few knew that Operation Ice Castle was happening. We did our best to keep it a secret because of the high degree of risk involved. We do not feel the same need to keep our next large event, Operation Queen's Palace, a secret. Thus, this booklet and other public announcements will be made.

THE HIDDEN MANNA

Alice Smith's fax had prepared us to receive the "hidden manna," which would be a revelation of certain new steps to take toward completing Jesus' Great Commission to make disciples of all nations. This began to take shape when, as a part of our tour of Ephesus, we entered the 25,000-seat amphitheater where the riot described in Acts 19 was instigated by Diana's idol makers.

In the amphitheater, which was not too crowded at the time, I asked Doris and our Muslim tour guide to come with me to a quiet section where I wanted to conduct a ceremony. I took from my pocket a copy of the apology statement, in Turkish, being used by the intercessors on the Reconciliation Walk. Even though the crusaders did not come through the region of Ephesus, I still told our Muslim guide that I wanted to apologize for the sins of our Christian forebears, the crusaders, against his people. He knew exactly what I was talking about. I told him how sorry Doris and I were, and I asked him to read the statement in Turkish. He was visibly moved, and he said that on behalf of his people he would forgive us.

As this was taking place, God spoke to me and showed me that one day this very amphitheater would hold a multitude of Christians lifting praises to Jesus. It was the beginning of the hidden manna revelation.

THE KITCHEN COUNTER REVELATION
OF OPERATION QUEEN'S PALACE

The next part came when Cindy Jacobs, who is one of our I-2 intercessors, visited our home in Colorado Springs on Labor Day. We were standing in our kitchen debriefing. We told her what we had found in Turkey, and that it was one of the few countries to which, when we left, we strongly wanted to return. We showed her a map where some think the Garden of Eden was located and

Mt. Ararat where Noah's ark landed and Antioch and Tarsus and the Seven Churches of Revelation and Iconium, Lystra and Derbe and Tarsus and the Island of Patmos and many other places in the region where biblical Christians have spiritual roots.

Then we showed her pictures of Diana, the ruins of her temple, the idol of Mary and other things related to the Queen of Heaven. As we spread out the maps on the kitchen counter and conversed, the Holy Spirit seemed to descend in power. Cindy, in a tone she frequently reserves for prophetic words, said, "For years the Spiritual Warfare Network has launched skirmishes against strongholds of the Queen of Heaven in many parts of the world. It's time now to call the troops together from every continent and move into her palace!" Doris and I sensed instant agreement. My mind went back to the "hidden manna" I was to receive, and I felt this must be related to it.

I felt that we were in one of those moments that Paul prayed for in Ephesians 1:17: "that the God of our Lord Jesus Christ, the Father of glory, may give to you the spirit of wisdom and revelation in the knowledge of Him." Wisdom and revelation were coming very rapidly.

When should we do this? Operation Ice Castle ended the week before Praying Through the Window III in October 1997. Operation Queen's Palace should take place two years later, just before Praying Through the Window IV in October 1999. Therefore, we should schedule it during the last week in September 1999.

WORLDWIDE SPIRITUAL MAPPING

I pictured George Otis, Jr., the head of our Spiritual Mapping Division, coordinating a massive amount of research. He could locate at least 50 sites in Turkey and possibly in adjacent nations as well which prayer journey teams from all continents would visit and pray. Since then, he has agreed that his Sentinel Group will prepare a full-color prayer map of the region to guide the on-site intercessors.

I pictured Beverly Pegues of the Christian Information Network coordinating hundreds, possibly thousands, of prayer journeyers on the computer databases that she uses to coordinate the Praying

Through the Window efforts. She has agreed. By that time, we hope to be moved into the new World Prayer Center in Colorado Springs.

As we discussed it, we felt that Turkey should be the central focus of our prayers, but that simultaneously prophetic intercessors around the world should plan prayer actions at the major power points of the Queen of Heaven in as many other countries as possible, especially the countries sending prayer journeyers to Turkey. This will require careful spiritual mapping all over the world. Neuza Itioka, Spiritual Warfare Network coordinator for Brazil, says that the Queen of Heaven's major manifestation in their country is the Virgin Aparecida, and that they already know where her five major power points are located. Nozomu Takimoto, the chief spiritual mapper of Japan, has located the five major footholds of Amaterasu Omikami, the Sun Goddess. Some of our people in England say they have information indicating how Stonehenge is related. Huge amounts of information will be coming in over the months, and we will collect it in the World Prayer Center and make it available on the Internet and on the World Wide Web.

This means that intercessors, using the spiritual equipment that has become so well known during this decade, will be attacking the forces of darkness on all fronts during the last week in September 1999 in hundreds of home-based assaults. The enemy will not be able to redeploy his forces to the extent he might wish.

Before we took any concrete steps, I called Bobbye Byerly and Chuck Pierce, who had led our Spiritual Warfare Network intercession team through the years. I wouldn't have gone any further if they were not in agreement. But both of them sensed a clear witness from the Spirit that this was, indeed, the will of God.

BACK TO THE AMPHITHEATER

While we were talking and dreaming and planning in the kitchen, my mind went back to the ceremony of identificational repentance and reconciliation with our Muslim guide in the amphitheater in

Ephesus. That is where God began to give me the promised "hidden manna." "This is it!" I said to Doris and Cindy. "When the week is over and our prayer teams have prayed God's blessing all through Turkey, we will all arrange our tours so that the tour buses will converge on Ephesus the last day. We will all make our way to the 25,000-seat amphitheater where the devotees of the Queen of Heaven shouted 'Great is Diana of the Ephesians' for two hours (see Acts 19:34). There we will declare in one accord, 'Great is Jesus of Nazareth,' for four hours!"

Ted Haggard, senior pastor of New Life Church in Colorado Springs, has agreed to be the conference pastor for the event. Worship leaders Ross Parsley of New Life Church and David Morris of Springs Harvest Fellowship have agreed to develop the four-hour program. There will be no preaching, teaching, or exhortation. There will be no overt spiritual warfare—it will all be done by then. We will spend our time in worship and high praise, prayer and Scripture. Outstanding Christian leaders from all over the world will take turns leading us in powerful prayers aimed at exalting the Lord and releasing His blessing on the unreached peoples of the world.

THE HALLELUJAH CHORUS

Soon after we decided to do Operation Queen's Palace, I found myself in Korea eating dinner with Bishop Kim Sundo, pastor of the 80,000-member Kwang Lim Methodist Church and Methodist Bishop of Korea. In 1993, Pastor Kim generously hosted 300 members of the International Spiritual Warfare Network in the church's luxurious prayer mountain facilities. One of the most memorable events of those few days together was the visit of the Kwang Lim Choir, which one evening presented a magnificent concert of classical Christian music.

I told Pastor Kim about Operation Queen's Palace. Then I said, "Pastor Kim, the members of the Spiritual Warfare Network agree that you have one of the most anointed choirs in all of Christianity. Would you consider sending a choir to Turkey in

1999 so they could lead the grand finale of the four-hour service in the amphitheater in Ephesus singing the Hallelujah Chorus from Handel's *Messiah*?" Kim dropped his eyes and prayed for about five seconds. Then he said, "I'll do it! How many can I bring?" I replied, "How many do you want to bring?" "One hundred!" he said.

What a blessing! A one-hundred voice robed Korean classical choir leading us in one of the most beloved and Christ-honoring songs that the Christian church has ever known.

Great is Jesus of Nazareth!

YOU CAN BE A PART OF

OPERATION QUEEN'S PALACE
(a.k.a. Celebrate Ephesus)

September 27 - October 3, 1999

If you want to participate with thousands of believers in the exciting prayer journey you have just read about, you can get started with the two steps below:

1. Contact the Christian Information Network for a list of prayer sites in Turkey:

Phone: 719-522-1040
E-mail: operationqp@cin1040.net

2. Contact your travel agent to organize your trip or call one of those listed below:

Global Travel: 1-800-321-7798
Guide Travel: 1-800-836-6065

If you have any other questions regarding this event, please contact Global Harvest Ministries:

Phone: 719-262-9922
E-mail: RichD@globalharvest.org

What is
Global Harvest Ministries?

There are still two billion individuals who are not within reach of the gospel and who do not yet have a vital, indigenous church movement.

Global Harvest Ministries, under the leadership of Dr. C. Peter Wagner, unites existing national and international prayer networks in order to focus maximum prayer power on world evangelization; especially for the lost people of the 10/40 Window.

Working with Christian leaders all over the earth, Global Harvest is **seeking to bring together a massive prayer force** that is equipped, trained and focused for the fierce spiritual battles that will free millions of people from the grip of the enemy, and allow them to hear and receive the Gospel.

We are seeking those who will join hands with us in the following ways:

- **In Prayer:** Mobilizing intercession and prayer for the world's most spiritually impoverished peoples.

- **With Financial Help:** Monthly support is needed to mobilize this massive, worldwide prayer effort.

If you are interested in helping in these ways, or would like more information on Global Harvest Ministries please contact us at:

Global Harvest Ministries
P.O. Box 63060
Colorado Springs, CO 80962-3060
Phone: 719-262-9922
Fax: 719-262-9920
E-Mail: Info@globalharvest.org
Web Site: www.globalharvest.org

WAGNER
I N S T I T U T E
F O R   P R A C T I C A L   M I N I S T R Y

Preparing Tomorrow's Church Today

The Wagner Institute for Practical Ministry was initiated in 1997 to be a catalyst to "Prepare Tomorrow's Church Today."

The Institute is being built from the ground up to provide quality training for practical ministry.
The emphasis is not just on events, but on a process that will lead to realistic implementation of the training provided.

Our goal is to see each member of the Body of Christ fully empowered and functioning in their giftings and callings. We are committed to excellence by providing the body with well-known leaders who will target training in key issues for the Church.

Dr. C. Peter Wagner

Please review the exciting upcoming conferences (listed on following pages) to see how we might help equip you in the Lord's calling on your life to advance His Kingdom. For any other information, please contact us at:

Wagner Institute for Practical Ministry
P.O. Box 62958
Colorado Springs, CO 80962-2958
Phone: Toll Free 888-965-1099 or 719-262-0442
E-mail: info@cpwagner.net
Web Site: www.cpwagner.net

1999 Conference Schedule

Jan. 8-9

Doris Wagner Deliverance Seminar
Dallas, TX
Call 1-888-965-1099 for information

Jan. 28–30

National School of the Prophets
Colorado Springs, CO
Call 1-888-965-1099 for information

Mar. 1-2

New Apostolic Reformation Mission Leaders Summit
Colorado Springs, CO
Call 1-888-965-1099 for information

Mar. 5-6

Doris Wagner Deliverance Seminar
Claremont, CA
Call 1-888-965-1099 for information

Mar. 11-13

Mobilizing the Church for the Harvest
Atlanta, GA
Call 1-888-965-1099 for information

Apr. 8-10

New Apostolic Reformation Summit
Colorado Springs, CO
Call 1-888-965-1099 for information

Apr. 22-24

Mobilizing the Church for the Harvest
San Jose, CA
Call 1-888-965-1099 For Information

May 23-25

Prayer Room Network Assembly
Colorado Springs, CO
Call 1-888-965-1099 for information

Jun. 4-5	**Northeast Regional Deliverance Conf.** Rochester, NY Call 1-888-965-1099 for information
Jun. 24-26	**National Worship Summit** Dallas, TX Call 1-888-965-1099 for information
Jul. 29-31	**World Congress on Deliverance** Colorado Springs, CO Call 1-888-965-1099 for information
Sep. 16-18	**Building Foundations for Revival** Miami, FL Call 1-888-965-1099 for information
Oct. 28-30	**Building Foundations for Revival** Portland, OR Call 1-888-965-1099 for information
Nov. 18-20	**International Conference on Prayer and Spiritual Warfare** Houston, TX Call 1-888-965-1099 for information
Dec. 1-4	**Int'l Intercessors Gathering** Colorado Springs, CO Call 1-888-965-1099 for information
Dec. 31-Jan. 1, 2000	**Prayer Vigil** Colorado Springs, CO Call 1-888-965-1099 for information

WAGNER
INSTITUTE
FOR PRACTICAL MINISTRY
Preparing Tomorrow's Church Today